I0407638

MAGNETIC MARKETING MAGIC (MMM)

10 Explosive Strategies to Captivate Customers and Skyrocket Sales!"

By
Robert K. Braun

Robert K. Braun

TABLE OF CONTENTS

3.3 Analyzing Consumer Behavior to Predict Trends

CHAPTER 4:Crafting Compelling Content that Converts
4.1 The Art of Writing Persuasive Copy
4.2 Creating Engaging Blog Posts and Articles
4.3 Mastering the Art of Storytelling in Marketing

CHAPTER 5: Unleashing the Power of Social Media Marketing
5.1 Leveraging Social Media Platforms for Maximum Impact
5.2 Creating Shareable and Viral Content
5.3 Implementing Influencer Marketing Strategies

CHAPTER 6: Harnessing the Magic of Email Marketing

CHAPTER 1:

INTRODUCTION - UNLEASHING THE POWER OF MAGNETIC MARKETING

Section 1.1: Why Magnetic Marketing Matters

In a world where attention spans are shorter than ever and competition is fierce, traditional marketing strategies no longer cut it. The key to success lies in magnetic marketing - a dynamic approach that draws customers in like a powerful force, compelling them to engage with your brand and become loyal advocates.

In this chapter, we will explore the fundamental reasons why magnetic marketing matters in today's fast-paced business landscape. We'll delve into the psychology behind consumer behavior and the power of emotional connections in driving purchasing decisions. By understanding these principles, you'll be equipped to build a marketing strategy that resonates deeply with your target audience.

Magnetic Attraction: The Science Behind Captivating Customers

To create a magnetic marketing strategy, it's essential to understand the science behind what makes people tick. We'll explore the psychology of persuasion, uncovering the cognitive biases that influence consumer decision-making. From the anchoring effect to the scarcity principle, you'll discover how to leverage these psychological triggers ethically to captivate your audience.

We'll also dive into the role of emotions in marketing. Research shows that emotions play a significant role in consumer loyalty and brand preference. By tapping into your customers' emotions, you can forge a genuine and lasting connection with them.

Crafting a Magnetic Brand Story

At the heart of magnetic marketing lies a compelling brand story. Your brand story goes beyond merely showcasing your products or services; it's about communicating your values, vision, and mission in a way that resonates with your customers on a deeper level.

In this section, we'll guide you through the process of crafting a magnetic brand story. You'll learn how to identify your brand's unique selling proposition (USP) and communicate it in a way that sets you apart from your competitors. We'll also discuss the importance of authenticity and transparency in building trust with your audience.

The Journey Ahead: Navigating the Magnetic Marketing Landscape

As we embark on this magnetic marketing journey together, be prepared to embrace creativity, innovation, and a willingness to think outside the box. Magnetic marketing is not about following a rigid set of rules; it's about adapting to the ever-changing preferences of your audience and staying ahead of the curve.

Throughout this book, we'll equip you with practical tips, actionable strategies, and real-world examples to illustrate the power of magnetic marketing. By the time you reach the final chapter, you'll be armed with the knowledge and confidence to create a magnetic brand that attracts, engages, and delights your customers, propelling your business to new heights. So, let's dive in and unleash the magnetic marketing magic!

CHAPTER 2:

BUILDING AN IRRESISTIBLE BRAND IDENTITY

Section 2.1: Crafting a Memorable Brand Story

In Chapter 1, we explored the importance of a magnetic brand story. Now, it's time to roll up our sleeves and delve deeper into the process of crafting a compelling narrative that leaves a lasting impression on your audience.

Your brand story is not just a marketing gimmick; it's the heart and soul of your business. It should convey the essence of who you are, what you stand for, and why you exist. To craft a memorable brand story, follow these steps:

- **Discover Your Why:** Start by asking yourself why your business exists beyond making a profit. What is the driving force behind your products or services? How do you envision making a positive impact on your customers' lives? Your "why" will become the North Star guiding your brand story.

- **Embrace Your Roots:** Your brand's history and journey are integral to its identity. Share the story of how your company came into being, the challenges it overcame, and the milestones it achieved. Humanize your brand by highlighting the passionate individuals who brought it to life.

- **Connect With Emotions:** Emotions are powerful storytellers.

Tap into your customers' feelings by illustrating how your brand addresses their pain points, fulfills their desires, or brings joy into their lives. A story that resonates emotionally will forge a deeper bond with your audience.

- **Be Authentic and Transparent:** Your brand story must be authentic and true to your values. Avoid exaggerations or false claims, as consumers today value transparency. When your story is genuine, it establishes trust and credibility with your audience.

Section 2.2: Designing a Stunning Visual Identity

Visuals are the first point of contact between your brand and potential customers. A visually appealing identity can instantly capture attention and create a sense of professionalism and reliability. Here's how to design a stunning visual identity:

- **Logo Design:** Your logo is the visual representation of your brand. Work with a skilled designer to create a logo that reflects your brand's personality, aligns with your story, and is easily recognizable. Ensure it is versatile enough to be used across various platforms and marketing materials.

- **Color Palette:** Colors evoke emotions and associations. Choose a color palette that complements your brand's values and personality. Consistency in color usage across all channels creates a sense of cohesiveness.

- **Typography:** Select fonts that are easy to read and reflect your brand's tone. Use different fonts for headlines, body text, and call-to-action elements to create visual hierarchy.

- **Imagery and Graphics:** Incorporate high-quality images and graphics that align with your brand's identity. Whether you choose photography, ill ustrations, or a mix of both, ensure they reinforce your brand's message.

Section 2.3: **Establishing Your Brand's Unique Voice**

Your brand's voice is the personality and tone with which you communicate with your audience. It encompasses the language, style, and values conveyed through your content and interactions. Establishing a unique voice sets you apart in a sea of competitors:

- **Define Your Tone:** Is your brand's tone playful, professional, witty, or compassionate? Choose a tone that resonates with your target audience and aligns with your brand's personality.

- **Consistency is Key:** Consistency in voice across all touchpoints, from social media posts to customer support interactions, reinforces your brand identity and fosters familiarity with your audience.

- **Speak Your Customers' Language:** Understand your audience's preferences and language. Speak in a way that they can relate to, using terms and phrases they use.

- **Empower Your Brand Advocates:** Encourage your team members to embody the brand's voice and values in their interactions with customers. When your team becomes brand advocates, it reinforces the brand identity in every customer touchpoint.

By crafting a memorable brand story, designing a stunning visual identity, and establishing a unique brand voice, you'll create an irresistible brand that resonates with your audience and lays the foundation for effective magnetic marketing. In the next chapter, we'll dive into understanding your target audience to create tailored and impactful marketing campaigns.

CHAPTER 3:

UNDERSTANDING YOUR TARGET AUDIENCE

Section 3.1: Conducting Market Research like a Pro

Effective magnetic marketing begins with a deep understanding of your target audience. Market research is the compass that guides your marketing efforts in the right direction. By uncovering valuable insights about your customers, you can tailor your strategies to meet their needs and desires. Here's how to conduct market research like a pro:

- **Identify Your Target Demographics:** Start by defining the demographic characteristics of your ideal customers, such as age, gender, location, income, education, and occupation. This information helps you create targeted marketing messages.

- **Explore Psychographics:** Psychographics delve into the psychological and behavioral aspects of your audience. Understand their interests, hobbies, values, attitudes, and lifestyle choices. This knowledge will help you connect with your audience on a deeper level.

- **Analyze Competitors:** Study your competitors to gain insights into their strengths and weaknesses. Identify gaps in the market and opportunities where your brand can shine.

- **Online Surveys and Feedback:** Engage with your existing customers through online surveys and feedback forms. Ask them about their preferences, pain points, and what they love most about your brand. This feedback can lead to valuable improvements and innovations.

- **Social Media Listening:** Monitor social media platforms to understand what people are saying about your brand and industry. Social media listening tools can help you identify trends, sentiment, and areas for improvement.

Section 3.2: Creating Customer Personas for Laser-Targeted Campaigns

Once you've gathered data from your market research, the next step is to create customer personas. Customer personas are fictional representations of your ideal customers based on real data and insights. These personas humanize your target audience and allow you to tailor your marketing efforts effectively:

- **Develop Persona Profiles:** Divide your audience into distinct segments based on common characteristics and behaviors. Give each segment a name, demographic details, and a brief backstory to bring them to life.

- **Understand Pain Points and Needs:** Each persona will have unique pain points, challenges, and needs. Dive into their motivations and aspirations to identify how your brand can provide solutions.

- **Craft Personalized Messaging:** Tailor your marketing messages and content to resonate with each persona. Address their specific concerns and showcase how your products or services address their pain points.

- **Visualize Your Persona:** Create visual representations of your customer personas, complete with images and key information. Display these personas in your workspace to keep your team focused on the target audience.

Section 3.3: **Analyzing Consumer Behavior to Predict Trends**

Consumer behavior is a critical aspect of magnetic marketing. Understanding how and why customers make purchasing decisions empowers you to predict trends and stay ahead of the curve. Here's how to analyze consumer behavior effectively:

- **Study Buying Patterns:** Analyze past purchasing data to identify patterns and trends. Look for popular products or services, peak buying times, and seasonal fluctuations.

- **Utilize Data Analytics:** Leverage data analytics tools to gain insights into customer behavior on your website and other platforms. Analyze metrics like click-through rates, bounce rates, and conversion rates to optimize your marketing strategies.

- **Consumer Surveys and Focus Groups:** Conduct consumer surveys and organize focus groups to gather direct feedback from your target audience. These methods allow you to probe deeper into their preferences and expectations.

- **Stay Updated on Industry Trends:** Keep a close eye on industry trends and innovations. By being aware of what's on the horizon, you can adapt your marketing strategies to align with emerging consumer preferences.

Understanding your target audience is an ongoing process. Continuously monitor and update your market research to keep pace with changing consumer behaviors and preferences. Armed with in-depth knowledge about your customers, you'll be ready to create laser-targeted marketing campaigns that truly resonate with your audience. In the next chapter, we'll delve into crafting compelling content that converts leads into loyal customers.

CHAPTER 4:

CRAFTING COMPELLING CONTENT THAT CONVERTS

Section 4.1: The Art of Writing Persuasive Copy

In the digital age, words have the power to captivate, persuade, and drive action. Persuasive copywriting is at the core of magnetic marketing, as it allows you to communicate your brand's value proposition effectively. To craft compelling copy that converts, consider the following techniques:

- **Understand Your Audience:** Refer back to the customer personas created in Chapter 3 and speak directly to their needs and desires. Use language that resonates with your audience, addressing their pain points and offering solutions.

- **Craft Attention-Grabbing Headlines:** Your headline is the first point of contact with your audience. Make it intriguing, thought-provoking, or emotion-stirring to entice readers to explore further.

- **Tell a Story:** Human beings are hardwired to respond to stories. Weave narratives into your copy that engage your audience emotionally and draw them into your brand's world.

- **Focus on Benefits:** Instead of just listing features, highlight the benefits your products or services offer. Show your audience how their lives will be improved by choosing your brand.

- **Create a Sense of Urgency:** Encourage action by using persuasive language that creates a sense of urgency. Limited-time offers and exclusive deals can prompt readers to act quickly.

Section 4.2: Creating Engaging Blog Posts and Articles

Blogging and content marketing are powerful tools for magnetic marketing. Well-crafted blog posts and articles position your brand as an authority in your industry and build trust with your audience. To create engaging content, follow these tips:

- **Research Thoroughly:** Ensure your blog posts are well-researched and provide valuable insights. Use credible sources to back up your claims and offer in-depth analysis.

- **Write in a Conversational Tone:** Aim for a conversational tone that makes your content approachable and easy to read. Avoid using overly technical jargon that may alienate some readers.

- **Use Visuals and Multimedia:** Incorporate images, infographics, and videos to break up text and make your content visually appealing. Visuals enhance understanding and retention of information.

- **Encourage Interaction:** Include calls-to-action in your blog posts to encourage readers to leave comments, share your content, or subscribe to your newsletter. Interaction fosters a sense of community around your brand.

Section 4.3: Mastering the Art of Storytelling in Marketing

Storytelling is a potent tool in magnetic marketing, as it creates an emotional connection between your brand and your audience. Stories are memorable, relatable, and help your brand stand out in a sea of competitors. To master the art of storytelling in marketing:

- **Identify Your Brand's Core Values:** Weave your brand's core values into your stories to showcase what your brand stands for. Authenticity in storytelling builds trust with your audience.

- **Use a Hero's Journey Narrative:** The hero's journey is a classic storytelling structure that resonates with audiences worldwide. Frame your brand as the guide helping your customers overcome challenges and achieve their goals.

- **Evoke Emotions:** Connect with your audience on an emotional level by tapping into universal emotions like joy, fear, or empathy. Emotional storytelling creates a lasting impact and fosters brand loyalty.

- **Feature Customer Success Stories:** Highlight your customers' success stories and the positive impact your brand has had on their lives. Real-life testimonials provide social proof and inspire others to engage with your brand.

By mastering the art of persuasive copywriting, creating engaging blog posts, and weaving captivating stories into your marketing, you'll create content that not only captures attention but also compels your audience to take action. In the next chapter, we'll dive into the power of social media marketing and how to leverage it for maximum impact.

CHAPTER 5:

UNLEASHING THE POWER OF SOCIAL MEDIA MARKETING

Section 5.1: Leveraging Social Media Platforms for Maximum Impact

Social media has revolutionized the way we connect, communicate, and consume content. As a magnetic marketing tool, social media offers unparalleled opportunities to reach and engage with your target audience. In this section, we'll explore the key social media platforms and how to leverage them effectively:

- **Facebook:** With billions of active users, Facebook provides a massive audience for your brand. Create a compelling business page, share engaging content, and utilize

Facebook ads to target specific demographics.

- **Instagram:** Visual storytelling shines on Instagram. Showcase your brand's personality through stunning visuals, use hashtags strategically, and collaborate with influencers to expand your reach.

- **Twitter:** Twitter's fast-paced nature allows you to stay current and engage in real-time conversations. Use concise and catchy tweets, participate in trending topics, and respond promptly to interactions.

- **LinkedIn:** LinkedIn is the go-to platform for professional networking. Share industry insights, connect with thought leaders, and use sponsored content to target business professionals.

- **YouTube:** Video marketing is thriving on YouTube. Create valuable and shareable video content, optimize your titles and descriptions for search, and engage with your audience through comments.

Section 5.2: Creating Shareable and Viral Content

In the realm of social media, shareable and viral content can exponentially increase your brand's visibility. To create content that spreads like wildfire:

- **Know Your Audience's Preferences:** Understand what type of content resonates with your audience. Are they more interested in educational content, entertaining videos, or inspiring stories?

- **Embrace Visuals and Infographics:** Visual content is highly shareable. Create eye-catching infographics, memes, and graphics that convey information in a visually appealing way.

- **Evoke Emotions:** Content that evokes strong emotions, such as joy, surprise, or inspiration, is more likely to be shared. Tell stories that tug at the heartstrings of your audience.

- **Utilize Humor and Memes:** Humor and memes can go a long way in making your content shareable.

However, be mindful of cultural sensitivities and ensure your humor aligns with your brand values.

Section 5.3: Implementing Influencer Marketing Strategies

Influencer marketing has become a dominant force on social media. Partnering with influencers can extend your brand's reach, build credibility, and attract new customers. Consider these steps for successful influencer collaborations:

- **Find the Right Influencers:** Look for influencers whose niche aligns with your brand. Focus on micro-influencers with engaged audiences rather than simply chasing follower counts.

- **Build Authentic Relationships:** Establish genuine connections with influencers before pitching collaboration ideas. Engage with their content, show interest in their work, and understand their audience.

- **Craft Creative Campaigns:** Work with influencers to develop creative and authentic campaigns that showcase your brand in an organic way. Trust influencers' expertise in creating content that resonates with their followers.

- **Measure and Analyze Results:** Track the performance of your influencer campaigns using metrics like engagement, reach, and conversion rates. Analyze the data to refine your future influencer strategies.

Social media marketing offers boundless opportunities for brands to connect with their audience on a personal level. By leveraging social media platforms, creating shareable content, and implementing influencer collaborations, you can harness the power of social media to fuel your magnetic marketing efforts. In the next chapter, we'll explore the magic of email marketing and how to use it to nurture relationships with your customers.

CHAPTER 6:

HARNESSING THE MAGIC OF EMAIL MARKETING

Section 6.1: Building an Engaged Email Subscriber List

Email marketing remains one of the most effective channels for nurturing customer relationships and driving conversions. In this chapter, we'll explore how to harness the magic of email marketing to deliver personalized and engaging content to your audience. Let's start by building an engaged email subscriber list:

- **Create Irresistible Lead Magnets: Offer** valuable lead magnets, such as e-books, guides, or exclusive content, to entice visitors to subscribe to your email list. Ensure these incentives align with your audience's interests and needs.

- **Optimize Your Opt-In Forms:** Place opt-in forms strategically on your website and landing pages. Keep them simple, and clearly communicate the benefits of subscribing to encourage sign-ups.

- **Segment Your Subscribers:** Segment your email list based on customer behavior, preferences, and demographics. This allows you to send targeted and relevant content to different audience segments.

- **Run Contests and Giveaways:** Organize contests and giveaways to encourage people to subscribe to your email list. Prizes that align with your brand will attract subscribers who are genuinely interested in your offerings.

Section 6.2: Crafting Irresistible Email Campaigns

Now that you have an engaged email list, it's time to craft email campaigns that captivate and convert. Consider these essential elements when creating your email campaigns:

- **Personalization:** Address each subscriber by name and use their preferences and purchase history to personalize the content you send. Personalized emails foster a deeper connection with your audience.

- **Compelling Subject Lines:** Your subject lines should be attention-grabbing and evoke curiosity or interest. Avoid spammy language and be clear about the value recipients will gain from opening the email.

- **Engaging Content:** Deliver valuable and relevant content in your emails. Offer tips, how-tos, exclusive offers, and stories that resonate with your audience. Use a conversational tone to make your emails approachable.

- **Clear Call-to-Action (CTA):** Every email should have a clear and compelling CTA that guides recipients to take the desired action. Make the CTA stand out with buttons or contrasting colors.

Section 6.3: Automating Email Sequences for Effortless Conversions

Automation is a game-changer in email marketing. By setting up automated email sequences, you can nurture leads, onboard new customers, and re-engage inactive subscribers with minimal effort. Here's how to make the most of email automation:

- **Welcome Emails:** Create a warm and personalized welcome email sequence for new subscribers. This is an opportunity to introduce your brand, set expectations, and deliver the promised lead magnet.

- **Drip Campaigns:** Set up drip campaigns that send a series of relevant emails to subscribers at specific intervals. Drip campaigns can educate, onboard, and gently guide leads through the sales funnel.

- **Abandoned Cart Emails:** Recover lost sales by sending automated emails to customers who abandoned their shopping carts. Offer incentives or remind them of the items left behind to encourage completion.

- **Re-Engagement Emails:** Revive inactive subscribers by sending re-engagement emails. Ask for feedback, offer exclusive content, or provide a special offer to reignite their interest in your brand.

Email marketing, when executed effectively, can foster lasting relationships with your customers and drive repeat business. By building an engaged subscriber list, crafting irresistible email campaigns, and harnessing the power of automation, you'll unlock the magic of email marketing to fuel your magnetic marketing strategy. In the next chapter, we'll explore the secrets of captivating visual marketing and how to leverage it for brand storytelling.

CHAPTER 7:

THE SECRETS OF CAPTIVATING VISUAL MARKETING

Section 7.1: Designing Eye-Catching Graphics and Infographics

Visuals have an unparalleled ability to convey information quickly and engage the audience on a deeper level. In this chapter, we'll explore the secrets of captivating visual marketing and how to leverage graphics and infographics to tell your brand's story effectively:

- **Consistency in Branding:** Maintain consistency in your visual branding across all marketing materials. Use the same color palette, typography, and style to create a cohesive and recognizable brand identity.

- **Simplicity and Clarity:** Keep your graphics and infographics simple and easy to understand. Avoid clutter and focus on conveying key messages clearly and concisely.

- **Visual Hierarchy:** Utilize visual hierarchy to guide the audience's attention. Highlight essential elements with size, color, or position to create a natural flow for the viewers' eyes.

- **Data Visualization:** Infographics are an excellent way to present complex data and statistics in a visually appealing manner. Use charts, graphs, and icons to make information more accessible and memorable.

Section 7.2: Utilizing Video Marketing to Tell Your Brand's Story

Video marketing has emerged as a dominant force in captivating audiences and leaving a lasting impression. Videos offer a dynamic way to tell your brand's story and connect emotionally with your customers:

- **Tell Compelling Stories:** Use videos to tell authentic and compelling stories about your brand, customers, or team members. Storytelling evokes emotions and fosters a deeper connection with your audience.

- **Variety in Video Content:** Experiment with different types of video content, such as explainer videos, product demos, behind-the-scenes glimpses, and customer testimonials. Diversifying your video content keeps your audience engaged.

- **Optimize for Mobile:** As mobile consumption of video content rises, ensure your videos are optimized for various devices and screen sizes. Mobile-friendly videos increase accessibility and engagement.

- **Interactive Videos:** Explore interactive video formats that allow viewers to participate or make choices within the video. Interactive elements increase engagement and keep viewers invested in the content.

Section 7.3: Incorporating Memes and GIFs for Humorous Appeal

In the world of social media and internet culture, memes and GIFs have become powerful tools for engaging audiences and adding a touch of humor to your brand's marketing efforts:

- **Stay Relevant and Relatable:** Memes and GIFs are highly context-dependent. Use current and relevant trends that resonate with your target audience. Humor that feels relatable is more likely to be shared.

- **Inject Humor with Caution:** Humor can be a double-edged sword, as it may not align with all brands' personalities or appeal to every audience. Ensure your humor aligns with your brand voice and values.

- **Avoid Overuse:** While memes and GIFs can be entertaining, avoid overusing them in your marketing. Use them sparingly to maintain a sense of novelty and avoid diluting your brand's message.

- **Create Custom Memes and GIFs:** Consider creating custom memes or GIFs that are specific to your brand and reflect your unique identity. Custom visuals can make your brand stand out in a sea of generic content.

Visual marketing is a powerful tool for brand storytelling and engaging with your audience on an emotional level. By designing eye-catching graphics, leveraging the potential of video marketing, and incorporating humor through memes and GIFs, you'll capture your audience's attention and leave a lasting impression. In the next chapter, we'll explore the world of search engine optimization (SEO) and how to boost your brand's visibility in search engines.

CHAPTER 8:

Navigating the World of Search Engine Optimization (SEO)

Section 8.1: Understanding the Basics of SEO for Visibility

In today's digital landscape, search engines play a vital role in driving organic traffic to your website. Search Engine Optimization (SEO) is the process of optimizing your online content to rank higher in search engine results. This chapter will provide an overview of SEO essentials to enhance your brand's online visibility:

- **Keyword Research:** Conduct thorough keyword research to identify relevant and high-traffic keywords related to your industry and offerings. Use keyword research tools to uncover valuable insights and target the right audience.

- **On-Page SEO:** Optimize your website's content, meta tags, headings, and URLs with the identified keywords. Focus on creating valuable, user-friendly content that aligns with search intent.

- **Off-Page SEO:** Build high-quality backlinks from reputable websites to establish your website's authority and credibility. Engage in outreach, content marketing, and guest posting to earn valuable backlinks.

- **Mobile-Friendly Design:** Ensure your website is mobile-responsive to cater to the growing number of mobile users. Mobile-friendly sites rank higher in mobile search results.

Section 8.2: On-Page and Off-Page SEO Strategies for Higher Rankings

To improve your website's search engine rankings, consider the following on-page and off-page SEO strategies:

Content Quality: Create valuable, informative, and engaging content that addresses the needs and questions of your target audience. Well-written and in-depth content tends to perform better in search results.

- **User Experience (UX):** A seamless user experience is crucial for both user satisfaction and SEO. Improve site speed, navigation, and accessibility to enhance the overall UX.

- **Local SEO:** If your business has a physical location, optimize for local searches. Register your business on Google My Business, include your address on your website, and encourage customer reviews.

- **Social Signals:** Social media shares and engagement can indirectly influence your SEO rankings. Share your content on social platforms to increase visibility and potentially earn backlinks.

Section 8.3: Embracing Voice Search and Mobile Optimization

With the rising popularity of voice-activated assistants and mobile devices, optimizing for voice search and mobile is becoming increasingly important:

- **Voice Search Optimization:** Optimize your content for voice queries by incorporating natural language and long-tail keywords. People tend to use conversational language when speaking to voice assistants.

- **Mobile Optimization:** Create a seamless mobile experience by using responsive design, reducing page load times, and ensuring all elements are easy to interact with on mobile devices.

- **Featured Snippets:** Aim to get featured snippets in search results. These provide concise answers to user queries and can drive significant traffic to your website.

- **Local Voice Search:** Focus on local keywords for voice search optimization. Many voice searches are location-based, making local SEO strategies essential.

By navigating the world of SEO, optimizing your website for search engines, embracing voice search, and focusing on mobile optimization, you'll increase your brand's online visibility and attract organic traffic from relevant audiences. In the next chapter, we'll explore the world of influencer marketing and how to leverage it to expand your brand's reach.

CHAPTER 9:

TAPPING INTO THE POWER OF INFLUENCER COLLABORATIONS

Influencer marketing has emerged as a highly effective strategy for expanding brand reach, building credibility, and connecting with a wider audience. In this chapter, we'll delve into the world of influencer marketing and explore how to tap into the power of influential personalities to boost your brand:

Section 9.1: Identifying and Connecting with Influencers in Your Niche

To launch a successful influencer marketing campaign, you need to find the right influencers who align with your brand and have a genuine connection with their followers. Consider these steps for identifying and connecting with influencers:

- **Research and Vet Influencers:** Conduct thorough research to identify influencers in your niche. Evaluate their content, engagement levels, authenticity, and alignment with your brand values.

- **Narrow Down Your Selection:** Focus on micro-influencers with a smaller but highly engaged audience. They often have a more significant impact on their followers and are more accessible for collaborations.

- **Engage with Influencers:** Before reaching out, engage with influencers on their social media platforms. Like, comment, and share their content to build a relationship before pitching your collaboration idea.

- **Personalized Outreach:** Craft personalized and compelling outreach messages to influencers, highlighting why you believe your brand and their audience are a perfect fit.

Section 9.2: Creating Effective Influencer Marketing Campaigns

A successful influencer marketing campaign requires careful planning and collaboration. Consider the following strategies when creating your influencer marketing campaigns:

- **Set Clear Objectives:** Define specific and measurable goals for your influencer marketing campaign. Whether it's increasing brand awareness, driving sales, or expanding your audience, clear objectives will guide your efforts.

- **Establish Mutual Benefits:** Ensure that the influencer collaboration benefits both parties. Offer value to the influencer, such as exposure to your audience, access to exclusive products, or monetary compensation.

- **Co-create Authentic Content:** Encourage influencers to create content that aligns with their unique style while integrating your brand's message organically. Authenticity is crucial for the success of the campaign.

- **Track and Measure Results:** Use trackable links and promo codes to measure the success of your influencer campaign. Analyze metrics such as engagement, reach, website traffic, and conversions to evaluate the campaign's impact.

Section 9.3: Measuring the ROI of Influencer Partnerships

Measuring the return on investment (ROI) of influencer partnerships is essential to assess the effectiveness of your campaigns and make data-driven decisions for future collaborations:

- **Track Conversions:** Monitor the number of sales or leads generated from the influencer's promotion using unique tracking links or discount codes.

- **Engagement Metrics:** Analyze the engagement generated by the influencer's content, including likes, comments, shares, and overall reach.

- **Brand Mentions:** Measure the number of brand mentions or hashtags generated during the campaign to gauge brand visibility.

- **Long-Term Impact:** Assess the long-term impact of the influencer partnership, including potential growth in followers, increased brand affinity, and customer retention.

By tapping into the power of influencer collaborations, you can significantly amplify your brand's message and connect with new audiences. Effective influencer marketing campaigns have the potential to boost brand awareness, credibility, and ultimately drive business growth. In the next chapter, we'll explore the art of customer engagement and retention, vital for building lasting relationships with your customers.

CHAPTER 10:

THE ART OF CUSTOMER ENGAGEMENT AND RETENTION

Customer engagement and retention are the lifeblood of a successful business. In this chapter, we'll explore the art of building meaningful connections with your customers, fostering loyalty, and creating brand advocates:

Section 10.1: Crafting Personalized Customer Experiences

Personalization is at the core of customer engagement. Tailoring experiences to individual preferences and needs makes customers feel valued and understood. Consider these strategies for crafting personalized customer experiences:

- **Collect Customer Data:** Gather data from various touchpoints, such as website interactions, purchase history, and customer surveys. Use this information to understand your customers better.

- **Segment Your Audience:** Divide your customer base into segments based on demographics, behaviors, and preferences. Customize your marketing and communication to resonate with each segment.

- **Personalized Recommendations:** Use customer data to offer personalized product recommendations and content that aligns with their interests.

- **Respond Promptly:** Be responsive to customer inquiries and feedback, whether through email, social media, or customer support channels. A timely response shows that you value their time and concerns.

Section 10.2: Building a Customer Loyalty Program

A well-designed customer loyalty program can encourage repeat purchases and turn one-time buyers into loyal brand advocates. Consider these elements when creating your loyalty program:

- **Reward Points System:** Implement a reward points system where customers earn points for each purchase. Allow them to redeem points for discounts, exclusive products, or special perks.

- **Tiered Rewards:** Offer tiered rewards based on customer loyalty levels. As customers reach higher tiers, provide more significant benefits to incentivize continued engagement.

- **Birthday and Anniversary Gifts:** Surprise and delight customers with personalized gifts or special offers on their birthdays and anniversaries as your customer.

- **Exclusive Content and Events:** Provide access to exclusive content, events, or sneak peeks for loyal customers to make them feel like valued insiders.

Section 10.3: Leveraging Feedback and Surveys for Continuous Improvement

Listening to your customers is crucial for understanding their needs and preferences. Utilize feedback and surveys to gather insights and improve your products and services:

- **Feedback Loops:** Create feedback loops through customer surveys, post-purchase follow-ups, and online reviews. Address concerns promptly and use feedback to make necessary improvements.

- **Net Promoter Score (NPS):** Implement NPS surveys to gauge customer satisfaction and identify brand promoters, passives, and detractors. Use NPS scores to refine your customer engagement strategies.

- **Social Listening:** Monitor social media channels for mentions of your brand. Engage with customers, address issues, and show appreciation for positive feedback.

- **Customer Advisory Boards:** Consider establishing a customer advisory board where loyal customers can provide input on your products, services, and future initiatives.

Section 10.4: Creating Memorable Customer Experiences

Above all, aim to create memorable customer experiences that go beyond the transactional. Exceeding customer expectations can leave a lasting impression and drive brand loyalty:

- **Surprise and Delight:** Surprise customers with unexpected perks, handwritten thank-you notes, or personalized gifts to create memorable moments.

- **Go the Extra Mile:** Offer exceptional customer service and go the extra mile to resolve issues promptly and courteously.

- **Storytelling and Brand Purpose:** Share your brand's story and purpose to create an emotional connection with customers. Demonstrate how your brand makes a positive impact on their lives.

- **Continuous Improvement:** Continuously gather feedback and data to refine your customer engagement strategies. Embrace a culture of constant improvement and adaptability.

By mastering the art of customer engagement and retention, you can foster loyalty, build brand advocates, and cultivate long-lasting relationships with your customers. A customer-centric approach will not only drive repeat business but also position your brand as a trusted and beloved part of their lives. In conclusion, embracing the principles of magnetic marketing, harnessing the power of visual content, and leveraging influencer collaborations and customer engagement will propel your brand to new heights of success in today's dynamic business landscape. Remember, magnetic marketing is an ongoing journey, and staying attuned to your customers' needs and preferences will always be the key to maintaining a magnetic brand.

CHAPTER 11:

ANALYZING AND OPTIMIZING YOUR MARKETING CAMPAIGNS

In the fast-paced world of magnetic marketing, analyzing and optimizing your campaigns is essential for achieving sustained success. In this chapter, we'll explore the importance of data-driven marketing decisions, the use of analytics to measure success and identify opportunities, and the power of A/B testing for continuous improvement:

Section 12.1: The Importance of Data-Driven Marketing Decisions

Data is the cornerstone of effective marketing strategies. Making informed decisions based on data ensures that your efforts align with customer preferences and yield measurable results:

- **Collecting Relevant Data:** Identify key performance indicators (KPIs) specific to your marketing goals and collect data from various sources, such as website analytics, social media insights, and customer surveys.

- **Understanding Customer Behavior:** Analyze customer data to gain insights into their behavior, preferences, and pain points. Understanding your audience allows you to tailor your marketing to their needs.

- **Identifying Trends and Patterns:** Use data analysis to spot trends and patterns in customer interactions. This information can inform your content creation and campaign strategies.

Section 12.2: Using Analytics to Measure Success and Identify Opportunities

Marketing analytics is the compass that guides your strategic decisions. Leverage analytics to evaluate the performance of your campaigns and identify areas for improvement:

- **Tracking Key Metrics:** Monitor the performance of your marketing campaigns based on KPIs such as website traffic, conversion rates, click-through rates, and customer engagement.

- **Conversion Funnel Analysis:** Evaluate your conversion funnel to identify potential drop-off points and optimize the customer journey for maximum conversions.

- **Attribution Modeling:** Use attribution modeling to understand which marketing channels and touchpoints contribute most significantly to conversions.

- **Customer Lifetime Value (CLV):** Calculate CLV to assess the long-term value of your customers and allocate marketing resources accordingly.

Section 12.3: A/B Testing for Continuous Improvement

A/B testing, also known as split testing, is a powerful technique to optimize your marketing efforts and drive better results:

- **Experimentation:** Conduct A/B tests on various elements of your marketing campaigns, such as email subject lines, call-to-action buttons, landing page designs, and ad copies.

- **Control and Variants:** Create two or more variants (A, B, C, etc.) with one element changed in each variant while keeping the rest of the campaign identical (control). Compare the performance of each variant to determine the most effective approach.

- **Sample Size and Duration:** Ensure your sample size is large enough to draw statistically significant conclusions. Let your tests run long enough to capture sufficient data for analysis.

- **Iterative Process:** Continuously run A/B tests and apply the insights gained to optimize your marketing campaigns incrementally.

Section 12.4: Leveraging Marketing Automation for Efficiency

Marketing automation can streamline your processes and enhance the effectiveness of your campaigns:

- **Personalization and Segmentation:** Use marketing automation tools to deliver personalized content and segment your audience based on their preferences and behavior.

- **Lead Nurturing:** Set up automated email sequences to nurture leads through the sales funnel, providing relevant content at each stage.

- **Automated Reporting:** Automate data reporting to save time and gain real-time insights into campaign performance.

By adopting a data-driven approach, leveraging analytics to measure success, and conducting A/B tests for continuous improvement, you can fine-tune your marketing campaigns and drive exceptional results. The combination of marketing automation and data insights will propel your magnetic marketing strategy forward, ensuring that your brand remains relevant, engaging, and irresistible to your target audience. As you embark on this journey of optimization and growth, remember that magnetic marketing is a dynamic process that demands agility and adaptability. Analyze, optimize, and innovate continuously to secure a magnetic future for your brand.

CHAPTER 12:

GOING BEYOND BORDERS: INTERNATIONAL MARKETING STRATEGIES

Expanding your marketing efforts beyond borders can unlock new growth opportunities and connect your brand with a global audience. In this chapter, we'll explore the importance of adapting your marketing for international audiences, overcoming cultural barriers and language challenges, and the strategies for successfully scaling your business in new markets:

Section 12.1: Adapting Your Marketing for Global Audiences

Expanding into international markets requires a thoughtful approach that takes into account the unique characteristics of each region:

- **Market Research:** Conduct thorough market research to understand the cultural, economic, and social nuances of your target countries.

- **Localization:** Customize your marketing content, messaging, and visuals to resonate with the local audience, reflecting their values and preferences.

- **Regional SEO and Keywords:** Optimize your website and content for regional search engines and keywords to improve visibility in different markets.

- **Pricing and Currency:** Adjust your pricing and payment options to align with local currencies and purchasing power.

Section 12.2: Overcoming Cultural Barriers and Language Challenges

Cultural differences and language barriers can significantly impact the success of your international marketing efforts. Consider these strategies for effective cross-cultural communication:

- **Cultural Sensitivity:** Ensure that your marketing messages are culturally sensitive and avoid any content that could be misinterpreted or offensive in different cultures.

- **Local Partnerships:** Collaborate with local influencers or partners who understand the target market and can help bridge cultural gaps.

- **Language Localization:** Translate your marketing materials accurately and use native speakers to ensure linguistic nuances are preserved.

- **Visual Communication:** Utilize visuals and imagery that are universally understood and relatable, transcending language barriers.

Section 12.3: Scaling Your Business in New Markets

Successfully scaling your business in international markets requires a strategic approach and careful planning:

- **Phased Expansion:** Consider a phased approach to international expansion, starting with a few key markets and gradually expanding as you gain traction and experience.

- **Compliance and Regulations:** Familiarize yourself with local laws, regulations, and business practices to operate legally and ethically in new markets.

- **Customer Support and Service:** Provide reliable and accessible customer support to build trust and loyalty with your international customers.

- **Monitoring and Adaptation:** Continuously monitor market performance, customer feedback, and local trends to adapt your marketing strategies for optimal results.

Section 12.4: Leveraging Digital Platforms for Global Reach

Digital platforms offer powerful tools for reaching a global audience with your marketing messages:

- **Social Media:** Utilize popular social media platforms in different regions to connect with local audiences and build brand awareness.

- **International Influencers:** Collaborate with international influencers to expand your reach and credibility in new markets.

- **Localized Content Creation:** Create content that aligns with local interests, holidays, and events to resonate with international customers.

By embracing international marketing strategies, overcoming cultural barriers and language challenges, and strategically scaling your business in new markets, you can position your brand for global success. Remember, each market is unique, and a flexible and adaptive approach is essential for thriving in diverse regions. With a customer-centric mindset and a commitment to understanding and respecting local cultures, your brand can build a global presence that captivates audiences worldwide. Happy marketing on the international stage!

CHAPTER 13:

EMERGING TRENDS AND THE FUTURE OF MAGNETIC MARKETING

In the dynamic landscape of marketing, staying ahead of emerging trends and embracing innovative technologies is vital for maintaining a magnetic brand. In this chapter, we'll explore the importance of keeping abreast with the latest marketing innovations, preparing for the evolution of marketing technologies, and staying ahead of the competition with a magnetic mindset:

Section 13.1: Keeping Abreast with the Latest Marketing Innovations

As technology and consumer behavior evolve, marketing strategies must evolve too. Here's how to stay informed about the latest marketing innovations:

- **Continuous Learning:** Invest in ongoing education to stay updated on marketing trends, attending conferences, webinars, and workshops.

- **Industry Publications and News:** Subscribe to industry publications and follow marketing news to be aware of the latest developments.

- **Networking:** Engage with peers and experts in the marketing industry to exchange ideas and insights.

Section 13.2: Preparing for the Evolution of Marketing Technologies

Marketing technologies are constantly evolving, presenting new opportunities and challenges. Prepare your brand for the future:

- **Artificial Intelligence (AI):** Embrace AI-powered tools for personalization, customer service, and data analysis.

- **Voice Search Optimization:** Optimize your content for voice-activated devices and smart assistants.

- **Virtual and Augmented Reality (VR/AR):** Explore interactive and immersive marketing experiences using VR and AR.

- **Blockchain and Cryptocurrency:** Stay open to the potential applications of blockchain technology in marketing and payment systems.

Section 13.3: Staying Ahead of the Competition with a Magnetic Mindset

In a competitive landscape, a magnetic mindset is a key differentiator. Here's how to maintain a magnetic brand:

- **Innovative Content Creation:** Continue to produce high-quality and engaging content that sets your brand apart.

- **Customer-Centric Approach:** Always prioritize the needs and preferences of your customers in your marketing strategies.

- **Embrace Agility:** Be adaptable to market changes and willing to pivot your strategies when necessary.

- **Build Authentic Connections:** Foster genuine connections with your audience through storytelling and transparency.

- **Experiment and Take Risks:** Don't be afraid to try new ideas and take calculated risks in your marketing campaigns.

Section 13.4: Harnessing the Power of Data and Analytics

Data-driven marketing is crucial for understanding customer behavior and optimizing campaigns. Leverage data and analytics to:

- **Segment Your Audience:** Use data to segment your audience and deliver targeted messages.

- **Track and Measure Results:** Monitor key performance indicators (KPIs) to evaluate the success of your marketing efforts.

- **Personalization:** Utilize data to personalize content and recommendations for each customer.

Section 13.5: Embracing Sustainability and Social Responsibility

In a world increasingly focused on sustainability and ethical practices, incorporating these values into your marketing can enhance your brand's magnetism:

- **Green Marketing:** Promote eco-friendly practices and initiatives to attract environmentally conscious customers.

- **Cause Marketing:** Align your brand with social causes to demonstrate your commitment to positive change.

By preparing for the evolution of marketing technologies, staying ahead of the competition with a magnetic mindset, and harnessing the power of data and analytics, your brand can thrive in the ever-changing marketing landscape. Embrace innovation, stay customer-centric, and align with sustainable and ethical practices to build a magnetic brand that captures hearts and minds in the future. Remember, magnetic marketing is an ongoing journey of adaptation, creativity, and customer connection. Happy marketing on the road to a magnetic future!

CHAPTER 14:

CONCLUSION - UNLEASH YOUR MAGNETIC MARKETING MOJO

Congratulations! You have embarked on a thrilling journey to unlock the secrets of magnetic marketing and discovered the power to captivate hearts and minds in the dynamic world of business. As you conclude this adventure, remember that magnetic marketing is not just a set of tactics but a mindset that infuses your brand with an irresistible charm. In this final chapter, we'll recap the essential elements of magnetic marketing and empower you to unleash your marketing mojo:

Section 14.1: Embrace Your Unique Brand Story

At the heart of magnetic marketing lies your brand story. Embrace your authenticity, your values, and your purpose. Share your story with passion and let it resonate with your audience. Remember, your brand story is what sets you apart from competitors and forms the emotional connection that keeps customers coming back for more.

Section 14.2: Know Your Audience Inside Out

Understanding your audience is the cornerstone of magnetic marketing. Dive deep into customer data, engage in conversations, and listen to their needs. A customer-centric approach ensures that your marketing efforts are tailored to meet their desires and aspirations.

Section 14.3: Create Valuable and Engaging Content

In a world inundated with information, valuable content is a beacon that attracts and retains customers. Strive to create content that educates, entertains, and inspires your audience. Infuse it with creativity, authenticity, and relevance to make your brand an invaluable resource in their lives.

Section 14.4: Embrace Visual Storytelling

Visuals have an extraordinary power to convey emotions and messages instantly. Embrace visual storytelling to paint vivid pictures of your brand's identity and values. Whether through images, videos, or interactive experiences, let your visuals speak volumes about who you are and what you stand for.

Section 14.5: Harness the Influence of Brand Advocates

Your loyal customers are your best advocates. Cultivate strong relationships with them and provide exceptional experiences that turn them into brand ambassadors. Word-of-mouth and user-generated content are potent forces that amplify your brand's magnetic pull.

Section 14.6: Leverage the Power of Influencers

Collaborating with influencers can expand your reach and credibility. Choose influencers whose values align with your brand and who genuinely connect with your target audience. A well-executed influencer campaign can ignite a magnetic spark that spreads far and wide.

Section 14.7: Embrace the Journey of Magnetic Marketing

Magnetic marketing is not a one-time destination; it's a continuous journey. Stay curious, keep learning, and be agile in adapting to changes in the marketing landscape. Monitor trends, embrace innovation, and seize opportunities to amplify your brand's magnetism.

Section 14.8: Measure and Optimize for Success

Data and analytics are your compass in the magnetic marketing journey. Measure the impact of your campaigns, analyze customer behavior, and optimize your strategies for maximum effectiveness. A data-driven approach ensures you remain on course towards your marketing goals.

Section 14.9: Cultivate a Magnetic Company Culture

Lastly, remember that magnetic marketing extends beyond external efforts. Cultivate a magnetic company culture that empowers your team, fosters innovation, and puts the customer at the heart of every decision. A strong internal culture reflects positively on your brand and fuels its magnetic appeal.

As you unleash your magnetic marketing mojo, always remember that the essence of this approach lies in creating meaningful connections, providing exceptional value, and resonating with your audience on a deep and emotional level. Embrace your unique identity, amplify your brand's allure, and forge lasting relationships that transform customers into devoted fans. You hold the power to create a magnetic force that draws people towards your brand, and with that power, the possibilities are limitless. Happy marketing, and may your brand's magnetic mojo shine brightly in the hearts and minds of your audience!

Thanks, share and comment